LINDA McCARTNEY

Sun Prints

SELF PORTRAIT

LINDA McCARTNEY

Sun Prints

FOREWORD BY LINDA McCARTNEY

INTRODUCTION BY ROBERT LASSAM

BARRIE & JENKINS

LONDON

First published in Great Britain in 1988 by
Barrie & Jenkins Ltd
289 Westbourne Grove
London W11 2QA

British Library Cataloguing in Publication Data
McCartney, Linda
    Linda McCartney's sun prints.
    1. American photography, 1950- – Collections
    from individual artists
    1. Title
    779'.092'4
ISBN 0-7126-2141-5

Designed by Roger Huggett
Typeset by SX Composing Ltd, Rayleigh, Essex
Colour separation by Adroit Photo Litho
Printed and bound in Spain by Graficas Estella, Navarra

CONTENTS

PUSSY WILLOW

FOREWORD

I FIRST BECAME interested in old printing processes when I was living and working as a freelance photographer in New York. I used to spend a lot of time in the Museum of Modern Art where the curator at that time, Alfred Steichen, put on a series of exhibitions of historic photographs which really excited me. Not only were the photographs wonderful, the printing was better than anything I had seen before. The prints had a marvellous etched quality which I immediately wanted to achieve with my own photographs.

Initially I got nowhere when I asked photographic printers if they would help me experiment with old printing processes. I was told that I would need to speak to a chemist and that modern paper was not of good enough quality, being adulterated with synthetic ingredients. But not long afterwards I was introduced to Andra Nelki, a printer who shared my fascination with these old printing processes. Almost at once we started experimenting with sun printing.

Mixing the minerals and salts needed for sun printing is a bit like making a cake. Different ingredients and differing proportions of each in the mixture will give different results, as will different types of paper. You have to have fine, rag paper and we have found and experimented with a wide variety of wonderful hand-made papers to achieve different effects. We started off working in my daughter's bathroom, using the bath to wash the paper free of residual salts. This is one of the other aspects of sun printing which appeals to me. You can do it at home, you don't need a darkroom, a safety light or an enlarger and you're working with raw minerals, not chemicals. It seems to me to be a more natural process, using uncomplicated ingredients and natural daylight to produce an image.

Having said that, sun printing is nothing without a good image. You need a good strong photograph and a thick contrasty negative to get the best results. What I really enjoy is trying to get the most out of a negative. When I have an image I really love I will experiment in all sorts of ways to get the utmost final print. Sun printing has its drawbacks, such as loss of detail, and I am concentrating now on other processes to get even more detail into the prints.

The quality of light, too, makes a huge difference to the end result. We've worked at all times of the year, on hazy days, clear days, damp days and dry days. Spring and summer are best, of course, but sometimes you get the most unexpected results on a day which you might think would not be good. In producing some of the prints for this book we had to work between December and February, the worst time of year in England for daylight of any kind! We decided to experiment in another way, bought a cheap home sunlamp and tried printing with it. The results were fascinating: the blue cyanotype prints worked very well, but the brown, silver-nitrate prints were not at all successful.

A sun print is naturally always the same size as the negative used to produce it. When I first started experimenting with the process I only used photographs taken on my 10″×8″ camera because it has a good-sized large negative. The sun prints one sees from the nineteenth century all have a similar static feel because of the long exposure necessary at that time to produce a photograph. Even though I have been told that I use my 10″×8″ camera almost like a 35mm camera, moving it quickly from spot to spot to capture a fleeting image, I still feel it is quite limiting because of the short depth of field and the enormous amount of light needed. Recently I have been making sun prints of photographs taken on 35mm and 2¼″ cameras, first enlarging the negative to the final size I want. These pictures, such as those on pages 26 to 29, have a spontaneous quality which is quite unlike a nineteenth-century print.

A unique feature of sun printing is the pattern of brush strokes created around the edges of the image. When preparing the paper for developing you brush it with a solution of silver nitrate and distilled water, ensuring that the entire surface covered by the negative is covered with the mixture. Because the silver solution is colourless, the pattern made by the brush strokes is invisible until the print emerges and the results can be quite exciting. It wasn't long before I realized the creative possibilities of these brush strokes, if put on in a painterly way. Often I don't want the pattern created by them to intrude on the final image but occasionally, as in the images on pages 62 and 63, it is fun to use the way in which you brush on the solution to create a different type of image altogether. The combination of photography and painting has always appealed to me, particularly in the work of Robert Rauschenberg. It is a mixed-media technique I have experimented with before, but I feel with these sun prints I have come close to capturing the effect I am seeking.

The images in this book are a selection of the prints I have produced since I started sun printing a few years ago. The process has great potential and I find that the more I learn about it the more interesting the results I can achieve. Nowadays the technology of photography is so advanced that really one can do anything. Using an old printing process gives a picture that special quality that I find so interesting. In the end, though, it is the strength of the original photograph which really counts.

Linda McCartney
Sussex, May 1988

10   MILL STONE

INTRODUCTION

ABOUT THREE YEARS ago four of Linda McCartney's sun pictures were seen at a mixed photographic exhibition at The Royal Photographic Society, Bath. As the Curator of the Fox Talbot Museum of Photography at Lacock I was delighted to see these pictures made by the method invented by William Henry Fox Talbot between 1835-39. Linda McCartney has spent a considerable time in experimentation with this process and with the equally fascinating blue cyanotype process pioneered by Sir John Herschel in 1840, to achieve a set of hand-made prints, a selection of which comprises the images in this book.

Although neither process is technically complex, the final result depends on a number of conditions: the chemical formula used, the exposure time, but above all the choice of paper to be coated. Many frustrating attempts may be made before a beautiful result is achieved, and in order to appreciate the work involved in producing the prints in this book it might be helpful to know a little more about the discoveries of Talbot and Herschel which led to these processes.

As a scientist, Fox Talbot understood the reaction of silver nitrate, which darkens on exposure to light. On January 30th 1839 he announced the results of his experiments in coating paper in this way in a letter to the Royal Society. This report was published under the title 'Some Account of the Art of Photogenic Drawing or the Process by which Natural Objects may be made to delineate themselves without the aid of the Artist's pencil'. Talbot was rightly very excited about his discovery and later in 1844 he gave fuller details in his publication *Pencil of Nature*, the first book to be illustrated with photographs.

In describing the leaf of a plant, Fig I in this book, he stated:

'*Hitherto we have presented to the reader the representations of distant objects, obtained by the use of a Camera Obscura. But the present plate represents an object of its natural size. And this is affected by quite a different and much simpler process, as follows.*

A leaf of a plant, or any similar object which is thin and delicate, is laid flat upon a sheet of prepared paper which is moderately sensitive. It is then covered

with a glass, which is pressed down tight upon it by means of screws.

This done, it is placed in the sunshine for a few minutes until the exposed parts of the paper have turned dark brown or nearly black. It is then removed into a shady place, and when the leaf is taken up, it is found to have left its impression, or picture, on the paper. This image is of a pale brown tint if the leaf is semi-transparent, or it is quite white if the leaf is opaque.

The leaves of plants thus represented in white upon a dark background, make very pleasing pictures, and I shall probably introduce a few specimens of them in the sequel of this work; but the present plate shews one picture in the contrary manner, viz. dark upon a white ground; or, speaking in the language of photography, it is a positive not a negative image of it. The change is accomplished by simply repeating the first process. For, that process, as above described, gives a white image on a darkened sheet of paper; this sheet is then taken and washed with a fixing liquid to destroy the sensibility of the paper and fix the image on it.

This done, the paper is dried, and then it is laid upon a second sheet of sensitive paper, being pressed into close contact with it, and placed in the sunshine; this second process is evidently only a repetition of the first. When finished, the second paper is found to have received an image of a contrary kind to the first; the ground being white, and the image upon it dark.'

This is the basis of sun printing, the same process which Linda McCartney is using today.

Fig. II *Ships in Swansea Docks*. Photograph by the Rev. Calvert Jones *c.*1846. (Lacock Abbey Collection)

Fox Talbot quickly appreciated that a vital step in the process was to stop the chemical reaction turning the print completely black. In order to fix the image, he tried a hot solution of salt. This certainly assisted the action and stabilised the image, but did not fix it permanently.

Fox Talbot continued his experiments and on September 20th and 21st 1840 made a great advance with his photographic invention by obtaining a latent image on silver-iodide paper. This method changed his system of photography. When formerly his exposures were in hours, now a picture could be obtained in minutes. The development of this latent image was intensified by the use of gallic acid and he made paper negatives, which were fixed at first with common salt solution but later, on the advice of Sir John Herschel, with sodium thio-sulphate (hypo),

as used today. He named his process 'calotype', a word derived from the Greek word *kalos*, meaning beautiful. Fox Talbot was a considerable classical scholar, so it is not surprising that he turned to the ancient Greek language for a name for his invention.

In January 1841 Fox Talbot outlined details of his working method to Jean Baptiste Biot, one of France's leading scientists, who gave an account of it to the Academy of Science in Paris. In a letter to the Literary Gazette on February 19th 1841 Fox Talbot described his reaction to the magic of seeing an image form on a blank piece of sensitized paper: 'I know of few things in the range of science more surprising than the gradual appearance of the picture on the blank sheet, especially the first time the experiment is witnessed.' Photographers

Fig. III Cyanotype by Anna Atkins *c*.1842. (Fox Talbot Collection of The National Trust)

still experience this same exciting feeling nearly 150 years later.

It would be inappropriate in this introduction to sun printing to give working details of the calotype process, but the positive image made from the paper negative would be a silver chloride print, previously described as 'photogenic drawing'. Today it is possible to create sun prints by coating paper with the same formula as used by Fox Talbot. Working details are given in Appendix A on page 94.

Others were quick to use the new calotype process to produce sun prints, particularly Hill and Adamson in Scotland and The Reverend Calvert Jones in Wales. The calotype system became popular for portraits, landscapes and architectural subjects. Britain and France became the centre of photography in Western Europe with Vienna in Eastern Europe. Even after Frederick Scott Archer invented the wet collodion process in 1848, which was commercially available in 1851 as glass plates producing negatives, the positive prints were still sun prints, and this method of printing continued after the calotype paper negative was superseded.

The prints made by Linda McCartney and shown in this book are partly created using a modification of Fox Talbot's process and partly using another nineteenth-century photographic development, Herschel's cyanotype or blue print iron process, invented in 1842.

Sir John Herschel, a distinguished scientist, was already experimenting with the behaviour of nitrate and bromide of silver towards the solar spectrum. Fox Talbot's invention of the photogenic process intrigued him and he developed

FIG. IV *The Chess Players.* Taken in Claudet's studio with Antoine Claudet on the right. Photograph by W. H. Fox Talbot. (Lacock Abbey Collection)

further aspects of photography in his own right, publishing in the Philosophical Translation of the Royal Society of London in February 1840 his paper 'On the action of Rays of the Solar Spectrum on vegetable colours and some new photographic processes'. Herschel's contribution to the understanding of the early processes of photography was profound. As well as suggesting that hypo sulphide of soda could be used as a fixer of silver halide paper, he realised that some iron chemicals were sensitive to light, particularly ferric ammonium citrate, and in 1842 he described for the first time his iron process. This used potassium ferricyanide combined with ferric ammonium citrate to produce cyano-types, showing both white lines on a bright blue background and the opposite phenomenon, blue lines on a white background.

FIG. V *A Fruit Piece*. Calotype by W. H. Fox Talbot *c*.1844-46. Plate 24 'The Pencil of Nature'. (Lacock Abbey Collection)

Linda McCartney uses Herschel's process and has produced many blue prints of landscapes, still life subjects and portraits, coating with her chemical formula a variety of papers. The writer had an opportunity of seeing all of Linda McCartney's prints prepared for this book. There were often six versions of each subject, some printed in blue, some in sepia, some on thick, rough art paper, others on thin, smooth sheets, some on hand-made paper. These reproductions are a selection of her total output and she continues to experiment with these nineteenth-century processes.

There is no doubt that the composition of the paper, the weights of the chemical used and even the acidity or alkalinity of the mains water used all affect the final tonal look of the picture. The working fomula is based on the original nineteenth-century one, although it may be slightly modified to suit modern working procedures. A suitable formula is given in Appendix B on page 96.

Her subject matter embraces a wide spectrum of images: landscapes, still lifes, portraits and spontaneous images aided by modern techniques and equipment.

Photographic portraiture is a difficult discipline to master as not only has a likeness to the subject to be achieved, but some feeling of character must also be revealed. This is captured in Linda McCartney's close-up studies, where she uses natural light for modelling the features. The portrait of John and Donna Hurt on page 45 is such an example.

As well as her love for her family, she has a sincere concern for the conservation of the environment and for animals. This is reflected throughout her choice of pictures. Her atmospheric approach to strongly patterned landscape often indicates a sadness that it will not remain unchanged in the future. Her still life studies are reminiscent of the subjects chosen by the nineteenth century pioneers, Demachy, Hugh Owen, Dillwyn Llwelyn and Roger Fenton. She sometimes leaves her coating brush marks on the borders of the prints, exactly as Fox Talbot did with his pictures in the 1840s.

Every creative photographer reaches periods of self criticism in reassessing their work, and the hard work in the preparation of this book may be an example of a personal plateau of achievement. We may hope that she will continue this

FIG. VI *The Open Door.* Photograph by W. H. Fox Talbot *c.*1844. Plate 6 'The Pencil of Nature'. (Lacock Abbey Collection)

17

approach to her photography and tackle other modern applications of early processes: platinum printing being one example.

It is not surprising that the beauty of the photographs obtained by Fox Talbot's photogenic drawing and calotype process and by Herschel's cyanotype method should have caught the imagination of photographers today. Fox Talbot invented the negative/positive process of photography in 1839, using paper negatives, and sun printing them on silver salted paper, and it is significant that Linda McCartney is making 10″×8″ film negatives, taken with her beautiful Gandolfi Field camera and producing hand-coated prints 150 years later.

The book deserves careful study, and Linda McCartney should be congratulated on her achievement.

Robert Lassam
Lacock, Wiltshire 1988

THE PLATES

THE DUKE

POINSETTIA ON TABLE

JANUS, JAMAICA

LUCKY SPOT IN DAISY FIELD

WESTERN SADDLE

SHADOW LEAPING

LUCKY SPOT IN SNOW

BLANKIT FROM BEHIND

TERRACOTTA HORSE

ORANGE

SPACE IN FLOWERS

MERDOCK

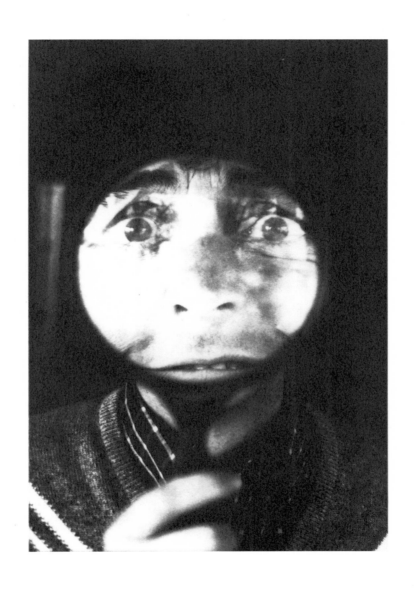

MAGNIFIED

36

EYEGLASS

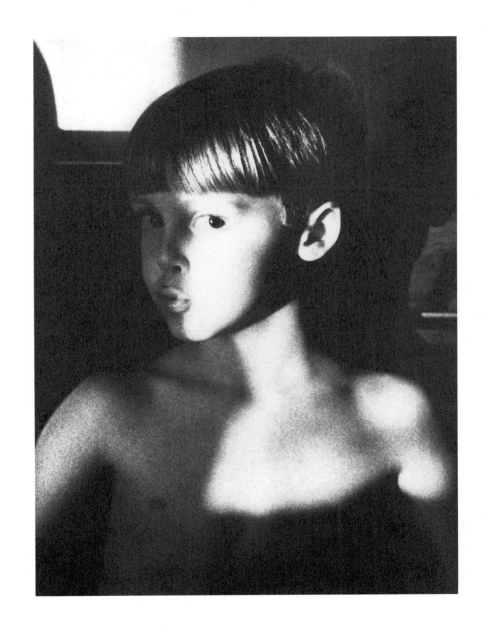

MONKEY BOY

EDDIE KLEIN

JOAN ARMATRADING

UB40

SELF PORTRAIT   43

TWINS

SCARECROW

GHOST

TERRACE IN SNOW

BODIAM CASTLE

BEFORE THE HARVEST

SHADOW IN THE PADDOCK

TREE TRUNK

THREE MEN OF WINCHELSEA

SAHUARO

THREE LANTERNS, WESTMINSTER

TAP WITH VASE

PUSSY WILLOW

GILBERT AND GEORGE

AUNTIE JIN

　　　　　MAN IN WINDOW

VALIANT, HASTINGS

EVENING

HASTINGS PIER

64   AUTUMN

WINCHELSEA BEACH

FOOTPRINTS

AMARYLIS

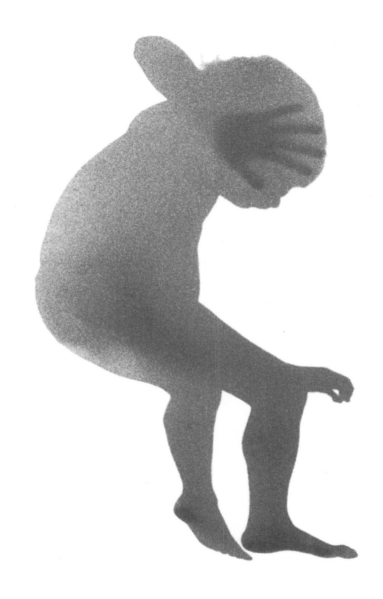

BOY SHAPE I

FACE PAINTING

BOY IN MASK

DOLLY TREE

JOHN SALTHOUSE

WRESTLER AND FRIEND

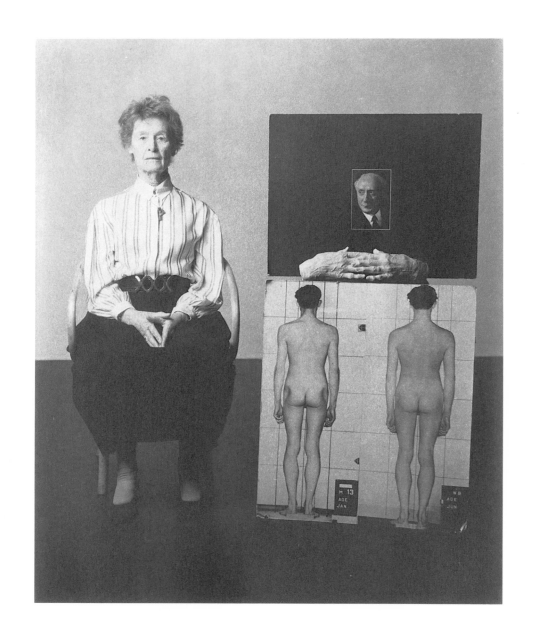

THE ALEXANDER TEACHER

STATUE WITH MANNEQUIN

MARY'S POT

JOHN HURT WITH SUNFLOWER

COALMAN

BRIAN CLARKE 81

LOVERS' TREE

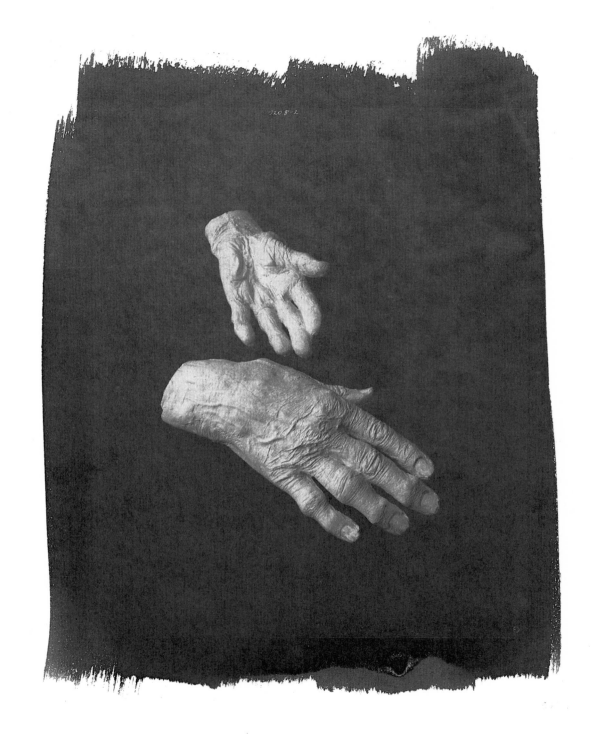

84   HEALING HANDS

ASTRO

EARL FALCONER

BLACK FACE SHEEP

SWANNY

STILL LIFE WITH VEGETABLES

SHADOW

STAINED GLASS

APPENDIX A

Photogenic drawing

You will need:

a) Good quality writing or drawing paper, strong enough to withstand thorough washing.

b) Salt (either cooking or table salt will do).

c) Silver nitrate (this costs about £15 for 10g which will make sufficient solution for several photogenic drawings).

d) Purified water (B.P.)

e) Photographic blotting paper.

f) Soft brush or cotton wool.

g) Photographic developing dishes.

h) Rubber gloves, which must always be worn when handling silver nitrate.

Making up the solution:

SOLUTION A. Make a stock solution of salt by dissolving as much salt as possible in 300ml of hot water. Allow the solution to cool and the excess salt will crystallise out to give a saturated solution. For use in preparing the paper, dilute 1 part stock solution with 18 parts water.

SOLUTION B. Dissolve 5g silver nitrate in 40ml of purified water.

Preparing the paper:

Note: Great care must be taken as the paper will become very fragile when wet.

a) Wash the paper in clean water to remove impurities left in it from the manufacturing process which might affect the result.

b) Immerse the paper in the salt solution and allow to soak for a minute or two, then blot the salted paper and allow it to dry.

c) In subdued artificial light and wearing rubber gloves, coat one side only of the salted paper with the silver nitrate solution. Use a soft brush or a wad of cotton wool and apply the solution evenly over the surface, then allow the paper to dry. It is now ready to be exposed. Because the solution is colourless, put a mark on the sensitized side of the paper to identify it.

The Cyanotype Process

Exposing the paper:

The silver nitrate combines with the salt to form a coating of silver chloride which is very sensitive to light. On a sunny day the paper will turn almost black in less than 5 minutes. Until required for use it should be kept in a light-proof container such as a black plastic bag used to protect photographic materials.

To make a photogenic drawing of an object such as a leaf, place the object in contact with the sensitized side of the paper, secure it in a printing frame or under a sheet of glass and expose the paper to the sun for 20-30 minutes. When sufficiently exposed, the paper should be removed quickly and put in a light-proof place.

Fixing the image:

To stop the paper from being further affected by the light and thus ruining the image, it must be 'fixed' by further chemical treatment. First wash the paper in running water until it stops looking milky. Then fix for 10 minutes in a solution of 10% hypo crystals and tap water. Wash for 30 minutes to 1 hour in running water. Pin up and leave to dry. You have now made a photogenic drawing.

You will need:

a) Ferric Ammonium Citrate (green).

b) Purified water (B.P.)

c) Potassium Ferricyanide.

d) Good quality paper, strong enough to withstand thorough washing.

e) Non-metal brush (a wooden or plastic pastry brush is ideal).

SOLUTION A.   Dissolve 20g Ferric Ammonium Citrate in 100ml purified water. (A good chemist will be able to supply purified water in 100ml bottles.)

SOLUTION B.   Dissolve 10g Potassium Ferricyanide in 100ml purified water.

Mix together solutions A and B in equal quantities. This mixture will not keep so ensure that you only mix enough for one day's use. Approximately 15ml will be plenty for three 10″×8″ pieces of paper.

In artificial light, brush the mixture onto the paper, coating it as smoothly as possible. Thoroughly dry the sensitized paper in the dark (the process can be accelerated with a fan heater). Place the negative in contact with the paper under glass and expose to the sun.

The coating on the paper will turn first green, then grey. The correct exposure produces a 'negative'-like image. At this stage, wash the print in cold running water until the desired effect is achieved. This washing will fix the image.

BIBLIOGRAPHY

Creative Sunprinting by Peter Fredrick (Focal Press, London, 1980)

The Handbook of Alternative Photographic Processes by Jan Arnow
(Van Nostrand Reinhold, New York, 1982)

The Keepers of Light by William Crawford (Morgan & Morgan, New York, 1979)

The Art of Photogenic Drawing by Michael Seaborne
(Fox Talbot Museum, Lacock)

The Pencil of Nature by W. H. Fox Talbot (Fox Talbot Museum, Lacock)

Photography Theory and Practice by Louis Philippe Clerc
(Isaac Pitman, First Ed. 1930)

Focal Encyclopedia of Photography (Focal Press, London, 1977)

Dictionary of Photography by E. J. Wall
(American Photographic Publishing Co. 1937)

A Guide to Early Photographic Processes by Brian Coe and Mark Haworth-Booth
(Victoria and Albert Museum, London, 1983)